Wigan Pier

An Illustrated History

John Hannavy & Jack Winstanlev

Smiths Books

Companions to this volume

Maypole, Diary of a Mining Disaster
John Hannavy & Roy Lewis
Pictures of Wigan
John Hannavy
both published by Wigantech Publications

cover photograph: Replica Wigan Pier with the Heritage Centre
& Canal Basin beyond: John Hannavy Picture Collection

Smiths Books (Wigan) Ltd

first published 1985
published by Smiths Books (Wigan) Ltd
41 Mesnes Street Wigan
telephone 42810/46270

text c.John Hannavy & Jack Winstanley 1985

Designed by Peter J. Kneebone MSIAD

Paperback ISBN 0 9510680 0 8

Printed by Ashworths Print Services Ltd
Peel Mills, Bury, Lancashire
Typesetting by Bury Phototypesetting Limited
Peel Mills, Bury, Lancashire

Contents

Acknowledgements

The photographs in this book have come from a wide variety of sources.

Our own private collections were the starting point, but the most striking pictures have come from Wigan Record Office, Donald Anderson, Mrs H Aldred and the widow of Arnold Hall. We are also grateful to British Waterways Board, Anthony Grimshaw, Cliff Webb and Wigan Newspapers Ltd, Fred Arnold, Ted Brownlow and many others for their advice, for information, and for the loan of pictures from their collections.

Thanks are also due to the staff of Wigan Reference Library, and the Library Service at Wigan College of Technology for their assistance.

Without the help of all these people, the story would be much less complete.

Particular thanks are also due to Marilyn Freear and the crew of Kittiwake, Wigan Education Department's floating classroom, for their help in producing the pictures of lock operation.

Under the heading "A Wigan Fairy Tale" a writer in the Manchester Guardian Miscellany column tells us that "Wigan Pier" is to be dismantled. That is rather like announcing that four o'clock tomorrow afternoon is to be thoroughly overhauled and painted green.

What do they know of Wigan Pier who say it can be dismantled? You might as well talk about spring cleaning a rainbow or arresting the Wandering Jew for loitering without visible means of support.

Wigan Pier is a deathless resident in the realm of original ideas — it abuts on the infinite and not on any mere material canal.

Let Wigan do what it likes with the iron structure that many people regard as the pier. The true, transcendental Wigan Pier of a thousand music hall nights is imperishable.

Wigan Observer, Saturday December 14th 1929

Introduction

The appearance of a book such as this — **An Illustrated History of Wigan Pier** — would have been unthinkable ten years ago. That such a book is now a reality — and available in the Wigan Pier Bookshop — is a testament to the sustained effort and hard work of many people who have fought long and hard to keep the canal-side buildings, to restore them to their former glory and to convert them into a major industrial heritage site. It is part of a growing celebration by Wigan and Wiganers of the town's industrial might and its past fame, or is it infamy?

To millions of people who probably couldn't tell you where Wigan is, and who have certainly never visited the town, Wigan Pier has represented a joke that they have been aware of all their lives. They may never have understood the joke, but they knew of it, and by it they knew of Wigan. Now the Wigan Pier complex will attract many of them to the town for the first time — to enjoy the warmth of a Wigan welcome, and to enjoy a walk through the industrial heritage of the North West of England.

We have had the idea of this book in our minds for a long time — and it is a particular pleasure to us that it's publication coincides with the official opening of the canalside complex.

Of course we have not managed to get hold of all the surviving pictures — there must be many which we have missed. Hopefully the publication of this book will stimulate interest in the photographic heritage of Wigan Pier, and other pictures will be brought to our notice. Any old photographs brought to us at the College — the School of Visual Communications is only just across the canal in Trencherfield Mill — will be copied and quickly returned to their owners, hopefully adding to a growing archive of visual evidence of Wigan's past.

What we have tried to do in these pages is to present a pictorial record of the canal basin and the site long known as 'Wigan Pier', together with a factual record of the history of Wigan's Piers, and a selection of pictures showing what life on the canal was like.

1. A Model of the Blenkinsop locomotive built by Robert Dalglish at Haigh Foundry which hauled coal trucks along Lamb & Moore's gantry from Meadow Pit to Newtown.
Photograph: Science Museum London

The Last Laugh

Wigan Pier is as much a part of British folk lore as the Loch Ness Monster. Mention to strangers that you came from Wigan, and they get that funny look in their eyes. You know what their first question will be, so you say "yes" before they ask you if there really is one!

The idea of a seaside pier, with candy floss, naughty postcards and Punch and Judy shows, in a town twenty miles from the sea certainly does conjure up an amusing picture — and, like it or not, it has made Wigan world famous.

It was George Formby Snr who popularised the idea — but probably not he who originated it. Given that Wigan was, at the time, the archetype of the Northern Industrial Town — with mill chimneys and pit winding gear the dominant features on the skyline — the idea of the town as a seaside resort was genuinely funny. Nothing could, in reality, be further from the traditional seaside town than late nineteenth century Wigan.

The Wigan Pier of the music hall jokes, however, was nowhere near the area which now bears that name. That original "Pier" was in Newtown, about two miles from the presently celebrated site.

There were, of course, several "piers" on the canal — coal loading stages at the ends of colliery railways. There is no evidence to either support or deny that these were called piers before the advent of the joke, so we cannot say precisely which came first — did the joke grow out of the fact that there were piers in Wigan, or did the coal-tipplers on the canal become known as piers because of the joke?

Whichever is the correct sequence, Bankes's Pier — the site now occupied by a reconstruction of the original tippler which was demolished in 1929 — became "Wigan Pier" as did the area immediately surrounding the nearby canal basin.

If Robert Taylor, one-time Station Master at Wigan Wallgate station is to be believed, the Wigan Pier joke started in 1891, when a trainload of miners was held up at a signal box outside the town. Across the often flooded moss, they could see the elevated railway which linked Meadow Pit with Newtown Pit. It certainly would have looked like the seaside pier at Southport, so recently seen by the miners on their day out. The connection was made, the joke was born and the train moved on.

Wiganers took a dim view of their town being held up to music hall ridicule — a pier where there was no sea, a pier where no boats arrived — but the image caught on and Wigan Pier was soon well known throughout the North West of England. As the Pier's fame spread, the townspeople had little choice but to accept it — and soon learned to capitalise on their new found fame.

Although the first Wigan Pier was a pier without boats, the adoption of the name for Bankes's Pier soon put that right. A wide variety of regular canal sailings from Wigan Pier were organised to local resorts — such as Manchester, Bolton and Rochdale!

In fact canal trips had been operated from Wigan since the early years of the canal's existence. Advertisements surviving for sailings as early as the 1820's to Wigan, Crosby, Southport and Manchester from Liverpool attest to that. The popularity of the service can be seen from the fact that at the height of the season, seven sailings a day were organised "to the fashionable resorts" while one per day made its way to Wigan.

Thomas Whitehouse's "History of Wigan 1820" records an announcement by J. Brinson, Agent Officer, Canal Wharfe, to the effect that:
"Packet Boats leave in Summer from Wigan Basin every morning at half past eleven and arrive at Liverpool at eight in the evening. To Manchester every afternoon at half past two and arrive at eight in the evening. During the winter months the packet departs at eight in the morning and arrives at Liverpool at five in the afternoon. Another Packet leaves Wigan each morning at six and arrives at Manchester at half past eleven o'clock."

An 1827 advertisement offered a daily canal packet boat service from Liverpool to Crosby, Southport, Wigan, Manchester "and intermediate places." The boats "possessed very superior accommodations" and passengers travelling to Southport "were attended by carriages at Scarisbrick and conveyed to Southport."

The advertisement further states: "By these boats, passengers arrive at Liverpool, Manchester, Bolton, Rochdale, Stockport etc., without the risk of the Tideway or the frequent accidents attendant on Steam Boats."

It is interesting to note, however, that these sailings were, at least until the turn of the century, scheduled to leave from and arrive at the Canal Basin in Wigan — with no mention of the Pier. As Bankes's Pier was completed in 1822 to service the Stone House Colliery, this does add fuel to the idea that the naming of these tipping stages as 'piers' is a twentieth century innovation.

In 1929, Bankes's Pier was demolished, leaving just the raised stone base on which the tippler had been mounted.

That ramp became the "Wigan Pier" from which pleasure craft embarked their passengers for cruises on the canal.

Coal traffic on the canal died relatively quickly — the railways taking the bulk of the traffic, although a few coal barges continued to use the waterway into the 1950s.

By the late 1960s the site was in rapid decay — and some of the ideas as to what to do with it were as silly as the idea of the pier itself. There was a sad period during which the listed buildings were allowed to deteriorate. They could not be demolished, but active preservation of them was not required by their owners.

Wigan's coal mines had gone — and Wigan & District Mining & Technical College moved with the times and became Wigan College of Technology now that mining was no longer on the curriculum. Of the dozens of major collieries that had made the mine owners of Wigan rich, not a single one remained. Many of the huge mills which had been fuelled by local coal had also closed. The Wigan Coal & Iron Company, one of the major employers of the area, was also just a memory.

For a decade it looked as though the pier area and its late eighteenth century and nineteenth century buildings would also go leaving Wigan with little tangible proof of its fine industrial past.

Then, apparently suddenly, but really as a result of lengthy planning behind the scenes, everything seemed to change. The idea of an industrial heritage project centred on the canal basin started to take shape. And where better — along the towpaths was, in microcosm, the fabric of Wigan's past glory. The superb 1777 warehouse at the end of the basin — one of the first buildings erected on the canal — was taken down stone by stone and rebuilt as prestige offices — with the impressive name of "No 1 Wigan Pier". The nineteenth century warehouses' too, have been restored for a variety of leisure and educational uses, and a Heritage Trail links the basin with nearby Trencherfield Mill with the largest working steam engine still in existence.

Now a walk along the towpath presents a very different picture. Wigan has done the only thing it could with Wigan Pier, and turned the fanciful idea of a pier — a place where people meet for enjoyment and entertainment — into a reality. Wigan really is having the last laugh.

2

3

4

2. The last coal screens at Lamb & Moore's Scot Lane Pit at Newtown, 1910. Here the coal which had been drawn along the elevated gantry — the idea for the original Wigan Pier of the music hall jokes — was graded.
Photograph: Wigan Record Office

3. **Wigan by the Sea — Sunset Pearsons' Flash** Once the idea of Wigan as a seaside resort had caught on, local photographers produced joke postcards celebrating the idea.
Photographs: John Hannavy Picture Collection

4. **Wigan on Sea** This postcard shows six views of Wigan with typical seaside postcard captions. It was produced by Blackburn of Wigan in the 1930s.
Photograph: Wigan Record Office

5. **Wigan on Sea** A variation on the same theme but without the sophisticated presentation, this composite postcard was also produced by Blackburn.
Photograph: Fred Arnold Collection

6. Looking towards the warehouse which now houses the Heritage Centre, this view from the 1960s shows the canal basin in a fairly derelict state.
Photograph: Wigan Newspapers Ltd.

6

5

10

The Douglas Navigation

Looking at the River Douglas today, it is difficult to imagine its strong practical link with Wigan Pier as the forerunner of the Leeds-Liverpool Canal.

Until the canal was built, the Douglas was Wigan's main — indeed sole — navigable waterway — and an ambitious and profitable one at that.

The commercialisation of the River Douglas is one of the most fascinating facets of its chequered history. It was carried out by a group of far-seeing local businessmen who launched a scheme to make the river navigable from its confluence with the River Ribble at Hesketh Bank to within a few hundred yards of Wigan town centre.

An Act of Parliament known as "an Act for making the River Douglas (alias Asland) navigable from the River Ribble to Wigan" was passed in 1720, seven years after a similar Bill had been rejected by the House of Lords.

The main aim was to expand the markets for Wigan's flourishing coal industry. It was natural, therefore, that the Commissioners appointed under the Act between 1720 and 1760 included various local colliery owners. Among them were Robert and William Bankes, of Winstanley; William Bispham, of Bispham; Sir Roger Bradshaigh, of Haigh (3rd Baronet), and after his death in 1747, his son Sir Roger (4th Baronet); Hugh Holme, of Holland House; and Edward Holt, of Wigan and Shevington.

As early as 1712, Thomas Steers, engineer and businessman who moved from Kent to become Liverpool's first Dock Engineer, surveyed and levelled the River Douglas from its junction with the Ribble to Henhurst Bridge on Chapel Lane. It is widely accepted, however, that the navigable Douglas ended at Adam Bridge which crosses the river at Newtown.

An interesting aside that gives an indication of the water quality of the Douglas at that time, tells of a clause in the indentures of apprentices working in a small factory on the river bank near Adam Bridge that "they were not to be fed Douglas salmon more than once a week . . ."

Alexander Leigh, a leading light in the Douglas Navigation project, recorded that work started in 1732. There were to be more than a few heartaches before the job was completed ten years later. Engineers and commissioners were replaced or died. In some instances work was delayed through a lack of interest and even after completion, banks, weirs, basins and sluices needed constant attention.

Even so, the Douglas Navigation brought a new dimension to Wigan's export trade and gave an air of romanticism to the Douglas valley in general.

The fee paid to Alexander Leigh for his work on the project was 63 guineas per year; apparently he was not in a hurry for his money, for on December 9, 1739 — more than 12 months after the job was completed — he submitted a bill for four and a half years' work. It totalled £283.10s.

The weirs and locks on the river were made from timber, mainly ash, and this was felled at Shevington, Standish, Parbold, Wrightington, Walthew, Hawkley, Bamfurlong, Hindley, and the Fairhust and Harrock Woods. Many fir trees were felled at Harrock.

Aptly, the man who did most of the tree cutting was Richard Fell, and one bill presented by him on September 25, 1740, brought him £4-6s-0d for work at Dean Lock, with £2-6s-0d for spademen and 2s.6d for drink.

Woodcutting was done with cross cut saws. Planks were produced in a saw pit by two men, one standing on top and another in the pit below. The rate for this was 11s. per rood — a rood for that purpose counting as 400 feet. Another job was snigging — the drawing of logs along the ground by horses and ropes after the branches had been lopped off. Payment for snigging from Dean Wood to Orrell Brow was 5s.

Timber was also used for the building of the narrow boats which operated on the middle reaches of the river where width was limited. Information on the size of those boats is sketchy but it would seem that they were about 30 feet long and six feet wide.

What is known is that they were "bow hauled" by gangs of men from Wigan to Parbold and Gathurst where cargoes, mainly of coal, were trans-shipped to sailing "flats" which sailed down the tidal part of the Douglas into the Ribble estuary and then out to sea to Liverpool, the Fylde coast and further afield to Milnthorpe.

Many boats were built for the Navigation owners, and their names included Resolution, Despatch, Speedwell, Supply, Success, Assistance, Concorde, Three Sisters, Three Brothers, The Laurel and The Pink.

Two other boats, built for pleasure, were named The Old and The New respectively.

The cost of building these boats is documented. A local man, Richard Roper, was paid £3-10s-11d. for a fir balk 45 feet long by 13½ ins. for a keel. One boat, Concorde, was built by Thomas Holland, whose first account for building the open "flat" on the stocks totalled £5-11s-4d. He received further payments amounting to £81-9s-9d.

Holland went to Liverpool to buy a mast, boom and bowsprit. The cost for himself and his horse came to 2s.9d. Other costs for Concorde included pitch and tar (£2-12s-2½d), sails (£42-5s-2d), rigging (£25-2s-9d), ironwork (£15-16s-4d) and painting (17s.11d). Concorde's lifeboat cost two guineas.

Other items bought by Holland were a compass, pumps, ash for the windlass, oars and tree nails. Why so much equipment for small boats plying a small river? The answer is that these vessels were sea-going, too. The men

12 The Wigan Lock

The river narrow boats at Parbold

who sailed them were referred to as masters and the boats carried between 34 and 44 tons.

Further upstream, the river was made navigable by means of weirs, locks and artificial cuts. There were locks at Wigan, Harrison Platt, near Adam Bridge at Newtown, E11 Meadow, Crooke, Gathurst, Dean, Up Holland, Appley Bridge, Gillibrand, Chapel House, Newburgh, Bispham, Wanes Blades, Croston Finney, Rufford, Ellerbrook, and Tarleton.

Having completed the navigation of the river, at a cost thought to have been £20,000, the proprietors, led by Alexander Leigh, set their thoughts on opening new markets for the coal they carried down the river.

Keen to recoup their outlay, they launched a sales promotion campaign in 1748, with adverts in the Kendal Press costing 5s. and "five several calls by the Bellman" through Kendal at cost of 1s.8d. It is not known what the Bellman called out.

Although coal was the main cargo, the boats also carried limestone and slate from north Lancashire and Westmorland on the return journey. Furthermore, there was a considerable trade in local grey slate, quarried mainly in the underground delphs at Roby Mill.

Other goods carried on this busy little waterway included pig iron from Birkacre, near Coppull, timber, sand, gravel, bricks, kelp (a coarse seaweed used in glass and soap making and the manufacture of iodine), tow (the coarse part of flax or hemp) and ox-horns.

A maximum toll of 2s.6d. per ton was fixed for all goods — except manure which was carried free of charge to owners of land within five miles of the river. Maintenance costs proved to be a burden and there is ample evidence of experts having to be brought in to mend weirs and locks washed away by floods. A quarry at Dean supplied stone for the locks and weirs. Crooke appears to have been the scene of some of the worst damage.

The Douglas Navigation scheme might well have reached further inland, for in 1749 there were thoughts of extending it to Hindley by way of Borsdane Brook. A surveyor was paid £1-2s.-11d. for testing ground levels from Pettycoat Lane in Ince to Four Lane Ends in Hindley but the idea was found to be impracticable because of a fall of 23ft. 4ins.

While bricks made at Tarleton and at Pool Bridge and Miry Lane, Wigan, were another commodity transported via the River Douglas, coal remained the mainstay of business. The Douglas Navigation was responsible for Wigan's famous cannel coal establishing a word-wide reputation.

Known as the choicest coal in England, this "black gold" burned so brightly that some Wigan householders used it to light their homes as well as keeping them warm. Much of it came from the Haigh estate of Sir Roger Bradshaigh and was sent "by the basket" to Pool Bridge for shipment. Cannel coal was sold in Paris in 1788.

All in all, the River Douglas provided a profitable outlet for coal from the Wigan area and more than a few individual fortunes were made on the strength of it.

Progressive thinking led to other businessmen laying plans for building the Leeds Liverpool Canal. It is, perhaps, ironic that the success of the River Douglas as a navigable waterway almost certainly spawned the idea for the canal that superseded it.

The Leeds Liverpool Canal was started in 1770 and the River Douglas Navigation virtually ended its practical life when in November, 1771, Alexander Leigh sold it to the Leeds and Liverpool Canal Company for £14,500.

Loading Orrell coal at Gathurst

Cargo transhipment at Tarleton

7. A heavily laden diesel powered barge pulls an equally heavily laden "butty boat" along the canal. The combined carrying capacity of this two-boat unit was one hundred and twenty tons of coal. This picture date from the 1950s.
Photograph: Wigan Record Office

The Canal

The Leeds Liverpool canal is the longest in Britain. To contemplate the construction of such a waterway with the tools and expertise of the latter half of the twentieth century would be to contemplate one of the most ambitious engineering projects imaginable. When we consider that the canal was conceived and built in the latter half of the eighteenth century — between 1770 and 1816 — with relatively primitive tools and only manual labour, the sheer scale of the project becomes awesome.

One hundred and twenty seven and a quarter miles of canal, twisting and turning, climbing and descending, link two of the largest cities in the industrial north.

Building began simultaneously at both ends — with the cut from Liverpool to Wigan, and from Leeds to Gargrave being built in the relatively short space of nine years. Those first stretches, however, were not built without some controversy — the original route of the canal missed Wigan completely. It was only the lobbying of local industrialists and colliery owners which convinced the canal builders to detour south and include the Wigan coalfields in the canal's route.

Work stopped after those first two sections were completed — and it was to be a further fifteen years before the monumental task of actually crossing the Pennines was undertaken. The "middle" section took a further twenty years to complete.

From Wigan to Liverpool — and on the stretches from Rufford to Tarleton, and Wigan to Leigh — standard barges can be used. For travel further eastwards from Wigan, the chosen lock dimension required specially constructed short boats to be built. The western section can take the British "standard" barge — with a 14½ft beam and an overall length of 72ft. For the remainder of the canal's lengths, only 61ft barges can be accommodated in the locks. While that did not pose any problems for the movement of the coal barges from Wigan, it did restrict the use of boats from the Midlands which might need to travel eastwards into Yorkshire.

It would be wrong, however, to consider the Leeds Liverpool Canal as a single pencil-line of water traversing the Pennines. For one thing, there were a number of spurs cut from the main canal. Two of them are in the Wigan area. The Rufford-Tarleton spur permits access to the River Douglas and then to the Ribble Estuary and the sea. The Leigh branch offers access to the Bridgewater Canal, and from there to the Manchester Ship Canal, and the Midlands canals.

The canal was, in fact, part of an integrated transport system by the early years of the nineteenth century. The Douglas Navigation — which is dealt with in much greater detail elsewhere in this book — had been in existence for years, making the idea of water traffic the accepted method for Wigan industrialists. Therefore, when the canal was opened to traffic in 1779 from Wigan westwards and north-westwards, it merely became an additional piece of an already well established system.

The coalmines in the neighbourhood had already established a network of horse-drawn tramways to bring coal to the Navigation and the various coal loading stages along its length. The tramway system was merely extended to deliver coal to new tipplers on the canal banks. The new waterway joined the tramways, the rivers and the developing railway networks as a complex and versatile transport system for the industrial output of the north west.

From Wigan's many coal tipplers or piers, the coal went either direct to Liverpool, or via Rufford to Tarleton, where it was transhipped to coastal vessels for delivery to Barrow, Liverpool and elsewhere. The use of Tarleton was probably, in part at least, traditional, as the port had been developed before the canal was built, catering for the traffic on the Douglas Navigation.

Only nine locks separate Wigan from the River Mersey at Liverpool — and eleven separate Wigan from the River Douglas at Tarleton. Traffic westwards was therefore relatively fast by canal standards — if passing through locks can ever be described as fast.

The coal barges which plied the canal between Wigan and either Liverpool or Tarleton were sixty ton bulk carriers. Only one of them could be fitted into a lock at a time, as opposed to two of the 7ft narrow boats which are often thought of as the more 'traditional' canal craft.

In Continental terms, British canals and the barges which sailed on them were small and narrow things. The standard Belgian barge, for instance, carries three hundred tons of coal as opposed to the 60 tons for the Leeds and Liverpool. Barges of that size ply the Aire and Calder Navigation to this day, feeding the giant Ferrybridge Power Station in Yorkshire. It was that relatively small cargo — coupled with the slowness at which it could move — which limited the lifespan of most of Britain's commercial waterways. The Leeds Liverpool Canal, however, was still carrying coal to the west coast until the relatively recent past — the 1960s — when the demise of the Wigan coalfield meant there was no more coal to carry.

If moving westwards from Wigan was a relatively easy matter, moving eastwards from Pottery Bridge presented the barge crew with a quite different proposition. Only the shorter 61ft boats could make the journey into Yorkshire, and immediately after leaving Wigan Town Centre, the famous twenty three flight chain of locks had to be tackled. To progress from one coast to the other, the canal presented a total of ninety seven locks and two tunnels. Of these locks fifty two were on the Wigan side of the Pennines — and almost half of them were encountered during the climb out of the town.

These statistics conceal one of the major factors governing the movement of goods by canal — the sheer time involved in getting through the locks, and, with a system of small locks, the waiting time involved in either allowing other boats through, or preparing the lock for entry.

However, despite the awesome amount of time and work involved, the transport of cotton, coal and a hundred other commodities by canal was less than one third as expensive as traffic by road. In the growing industries of the north west, moving sixty tons at a time by barge also made much better sense than breaking the merchandise up into three ton lots for road transport.

In the early days of canal traffic — and indeed well into the nineteenth century — the motive power was supplied by horses. The larger the barge, the larger and stronger the horse that pulled it! Given the sheer weight of the barges and their cargo, that meant that movement was relatively slow. Later on, steam power was introduced, and later still diesel.

This took two forms — single unit barges with

integral power units, or steam or diesel tugs pulling barges which had originally been built for horse-drawing. Horse drawn barges were a common sight on the canal well into the twentieth century.

After horse power was replaced by motor power, the barges themselves saw decades more life as 'butty boats' — powerless barges towed by powered boats. This system meant that well over one hundred tons of coal could be carried by one powered barge and a towed 'trailer'.

In short, a wide range of craft used the waterway and the locks. Every vessel passing through one of the locks used a considerable amount of water — at least 50,000 gallons depending on the size of the lock — and refilling the locks took a great deal of time.

When a boat travels up through a lock, the lock must be empty when the barge enters and full when it leaves. Descents require the lock to be full when the boat enters, and empty when it leaves. Efficient use of the waterway really depended on boats passing near locks. A progression of boats all moving in the same direction is expensive on water as each filling and emptying of the lock only effects one boat movement. If the boats could pass near a lock, each emptying and filling could permit two boat movements — one up and one down.

While it would be delightful for the bargee to find the lock in the condition he required it — ie empty when he was ascending and full when he was descending, that was seldom the case. Quite considerable periods of time were often lost waiting for the lock to fill, or empty.

Given a nominal speed through the canal system, when travelling on flat water, of two and a half to three miles per hour, and allowing the equivalent of half a mile's travelling time for each lock passed, an approximate passage time from Wigan to the Mersey can be arrived at — thirty five miles and nine locks being the equivalent of thirty nine and a half miles — about thirteen hours sailing.

Wigan to Liverpool city could be achieved in 9½ hours by passenger boats.

To Tarleton from Wigan — seventeen miles and nine locks being the equivalent of twenty one and a half miles — would take about seven and a half hours.

The twenty three lock flight eastwards out of Wigan — covering less than two miles — took almost a day's work to complete. After the six or seven hours it could take to reach the top, the bargees might feel they had carried the

barge up — such would be the strain on their backs of all the winching and winding necessary to work the lock gates.

Particularly in the days of horsedrawn craft, canal life was quiet. The boats silently making their way along the cut, sometimes loaded almost to sinking, offered a peaceful if hard working lifestyle for the people who lived and worked on the boats.

Along their way, they could pass through some of the finest countryside in the north of England. In the industrial centres, they passed some of the finest industrial architecture of the period — for many mill owners chose the prime canalside sites for their cotton mills, offering excellent transportation facilities, and a ready supply of water for the giant steam engines which worked their looms.

That tradition of marrying excellent manufacturing facilities and excellent transportation facilities is exemplified in the location of Trencherfield Mill — with its own loading dock, the canal water to power and cool the engines, and immediate access to one of the best transportation systems in the country. Within a matter of hours, the produce from the mills of Wigan and Leigh could be loaded on to barges, carried down the Leigh Branch to the Bridgewater Canal, Manchester Docks, the Manchester Ship Canal and the world.

The demise of canal traffic is a relatively recent thing — but when it did come it came fairly rapidly. Road and rail transport offered greater speed and versatility, leaving the canals neglected and unused. As recently as twenty years ago, with almost no traffic, the canal system seemed to be becoming derelict beyond salvation. Now, with the upsurge of pleasure craft, and the development of Industrial Heritage Centres such as the Wigan Pier complex, this stretch of the canal at least is being restored to its former splendour.

17

8. A 'short boat' at Top Lock. These 61ft boats were built specially to fit the locks on the Wigan to Leeds stretch of the canal. This one, registered No77 in Blackburn, belonged to Dean Waddington & Co.
Photograph: Private Collection

9. This unusual view of the ramp left after the demolition of Wigan Pier shows one of the last horse-drawn barges, complete with horse, moving slowly along the canal. Again, this is a short boat designed for the journey into Yorkshire. The picture also shows clearly the gap in the building line along the canal bank which allowed rail access to the pier itself.
Photograph: Wigan Record Office

10. At the top of the 23 flights of locks rising out of Wigan, the barge Everton is seen just about to turn into the old Lancaster Canal stretch and make its way north and eastwards into Yorkshire.
Photograph: Wigan Record Office

11. Some of the stretches of canal approaching Wigan cut through flashes caused by mining subsidence of long ago. Here a barge and butty boat are seen making their way towards Wigan in the late 1950s.
Photograph by Arnold Hall, Jack Winstanley Collection

12. An empty barge and a fully laden barge pass near Poolstock in the 1950s. The laden barge is trailing a rope, indicating that a butty boat is being pulled behind it.
Photograph: Wigan Record Office

13. Arrival of HRH the Duke of Gloucester at Wigan Pier during a Royal Visit to the town in 1934.
Photograph: Fred Arnold Collection

14. This photograph of a bargee and his dog on the roof of a canal boat was probably taken in the 1890s.
Photograph: Wigan Record Office

12

13

16. The boat examiner at Wigan reports to a family on the condition of their craft, 1891. The boat examiner was required to check the condition of narrow and wide boats, the types of cargoe they carried, the living accommodation and a variety of other things — such as hygiene. This is one of a truly remarkable series of pictures taken by the Reverend William Wickham, vicar of St Andrew's Parish Church at Springfield. The collection was recently acquired for the Borough Archives.

Photograph: Wigan Record Office

15. A horse drawn pleasure boat on the canal at Gathurst in the 1890s. This rare photograph shows that the canal was used for pleasure craft even in its busiest working days. The light structure of the boat only needed a light horse to pull it. The heavy coal barges required much greater strength. The photograph was taken by Joseph Hulme Aldred, an amateur photographer.

Photograph: Mrs H Aldred

17. Captioned simply 'picture boat, Wigan' this delightful Wickham study of narrow boat lifestyles is one of his acknowledged masterpieces. It is reproduced from a lantern slide, one of a number he produced in 1891 for a series of public lectures he presented in Wigan and Southport.

Photograph: Wigan Record Office

18

19

20

24

21

18. Canal boats moved throughout the country carrying their varied cargoe. This narrow boat photographed near Wigan c.1890 by the Rev William Wickham was registered in Coventry.
Photograph: Wigan Record Office

19. Christmas on the canal, 1891. The Reverend William Wickham took this fascinating picture for another planned series of illustrated lectures. Father Christmas is a representative from the London City Mission, giving out gifts to the children of boatmen.
The photograph shows a wide range of craft — three narrow boats, one with its covers off, are the most prominent, but behind them are a number of full size 60 ton coal barges.
Photograph: Wigan Record Office

20. Boatmen at Wigan Pier, a photograph from the 1950s with the now almost disused canal behind them. The raised abutment where the original Bankes's Pier stood can be seen in the distance.
Photograph: Wigan Record Office

22

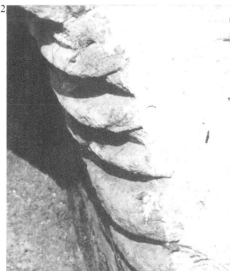

21. To assist the difficult manoeuvre of getting horse drawn barges under bridges, bridge rollers were provided. This reduced wear on the rope — but ultimately wore down the bridge roller!
Photograph: Anthony Grimshaw

22. Where there was no roller, the ropes took their toll on the bridge piers over the years.
Photograph: Anthony Grimshaw

23. Canal workers photographed in the late 1950s. Here we see a lock keeper, a bank ranger and two boatmen.
Photograph: Anthony Grimshaw

24. In the late 1950s, British Waterways Board employed diesel power units like this to push former horse drawn barges.
Photograph: Anthony Grimshaw

25. Horses were the sole source of power for the first years of the canal — and were still used as a power source well into this century. A fully laden barge was a fair weight — hence the size of the horse seen here with its handler at one of the many stables along the length of the canal.
Photograph: Private Collection

26. Pleasure trips on the canal were a common sight in the closing years of the last century, and the early years of this century.
Photograph: Private Collection

27. The "Water Witch" one of many boats which could be hired for passenger trips at the turn of the century. Here it is carrying Leeds and Liverpool Canal Company shareholders on an outing.
Photograph: Private Collection

28. "Tiger" was one of the horse drawn barges owned by the Leeds and Liverpool Canal Company and registered at Liverpool. This picture dates from about 1910.
Photograph: Private Collection

29. A heavily laden barge with a full load of coal steams along the canal between Liverpool and Wigan.
Photograph: Private Collection

30. "Beaver", "Amy" and "Agate", three steam powered bulk carriers owned by the Leeds and Liverpool Canal Company in the early years of this century.
Photograph: Private Collection

31. A horse drawn barge being used to carry stone for repairs to the canal wall and towpath, C.1900.
Photograph: Private Collection

Sailing through locks

The heart of the canal system is the lock — without it the canal cannot go up or down hills.
Ascending up through a lock is achieved by a simple series of manoeuvres.

(a) The barge is sailed into the empty lock

(b) The gates are closed behind it

(e) The gate paddles are opened — this allows water to enter the lock through openings in the gates themselves.

(f) The water level in the lock rises to equal that above the lock

(c) The gates are held shut simply by the pressure of water

(d) The ground paddle is opened. This allows water from the higher canal level above the lock to enter the lock via an underwater tunnel. From the boat all that can be seen is a great deal of water turbulence as thousands of gallons of water enter the lock from underneath. To allow all the water to come in through the gates would probably sink the boat!

(g) Now the water level in the lock is several feet above the canal level we have just left.

(h) With the top gates open, the boat sails out and continues the journey.

Descending through a lock is a lot simpler — assuming that the lock is full when you arrive

(j) The boat sails into the lock and the gates are closed behind it

(k) The gate paddles on the bottom gates are opened, allowing water to escape to the canal below

(l) The water level drops to equal the lower canal level and the gates are opened

(m) the boat sails out and continues its journey

Photographs: John Hannavy

Wigan's Piers

If we choose to use one of the many dictionary definitions of a pier — an abutment of stone or wood used as a landing stage — then the Leeds Liverpool Canal, and Wigan in particular, has had piers since the cut was opened in the late eighteenth century. In that respect, there is little practical difference between Wigan's coal piers, and Liverpool's ferry piers. The definition of a seaside or promenade pier — the one on which George Formby Snr built his jokes — is an entirely different matter.

As the holiday resorts' promenade piers originally developed out of landing stages — and most of them did have landing stages at the end of them — the two definitions are not really very different, although the pictures they conjure up in our minds are.

In getting to grips with the origins of Wigan Pier, we have two quite different things to contend with. Firstly, the image of the seaside promenade pier — as used by Formby — and secondly, the fact of the numerous small coal-loading piers along this stretch of the canal.

The original Wigan Pier of the jokes was almost certainly an elevated tramway linking two collieries owned by Lamb & Moore. Running for about two thirds of a mile, it linked the Newtown Pit with the Meadow Pit, crossing over the canal and the River Douglas on its way.

On wooden trestles, the tramway allowed coal tubs to be rope-hauled to the rail-heads near Frog Lane. The land beneath the gantry was prone to flooding — being rather lower than the river — and under the appropriate conditions, this gantry might indeed look rather like a seaside pier.

The gantry seems to have been built about 1889-1890, so would have been a relatively recent addition to the scenery when the trainload of miners returning from Southport in 1891 was held up at signals.

There is even a suggestion that a wooden hut housing the winding gear (the pier pavilion?) was sited on the tramway, adding to the visual similarity between Wigan Pier and Southport Pier!

At the same time, it must be conceded that there is strong evidence to suggest that at least some of the coal loading stages on the canal were already commonly known as piers.

The presently marked site of Wigan Pier may indeed have already been known as Bankes's Pier by the 1890s. Crooke Pier, too, may also have been commonly known as such long before the jokes started. But so far, we have not come across specific references to a Wigan Pier before the advent of the music hall one. Just when Bankes's Pier became known as Wigan Pier is unclear, but was certainly revelling in that name by the time of the First World War. The Lamb & Moore's Gantry was demolished some time around 1910, so the small abutment we now know as the pier may have adopted the mantle of fame very shortly thereafter.

The earliest coal loading pier in the area seems to have been built at Crooke in the early years of the last century. This structure, in a small village about two miles distant from Wigan, was used to load barges with coal from pits in Orrell. The earliest photographic evidence we have of Crooke Pier is in the form of photographic prints from the late 1870s — and it seems to have been a massive stone-built structure with a complicated tipping mechanism at the end of it. It certainly is on an altogether grander scale than the small structure we now celebrate.

Even in the 1870s, the Crooke Pier was capable of handling much larger coal trucks than the smaller Bankes's Pier. An ingenious system of counterbalances and winches — probably steam powered — tipped the huge wagons over the waiting barges below.

Twentieth century strengthening and reconstruction work on Crooke Pier changed its shape — replacing the heavy brick buttresses with smaller constructions — and a modified tipping mechanism was installed.

When John Clarke built the pier, and the associated tramways to link the John Pit in Orrell with the canal, he used a four foot gauge railway on stone blocks. Robert Dalglish experimented with early steam locomotives on the tramway as early as 1812, considerably speeding up the movement of coal. Nearby, coal was brought from Standish Hall colliery by barge through a one thousand yard tunnel — with bargees legging the heavily laden craft through two thirds of a mile of darkness. While the tunnel and the canal it carried were disused by 1850, John Clark's

tramway and pier were still in use one hundred years later.

There were numerous other tramways, railways and piers. Hustler's Railway carried coal from the Far Moor pits to a small tipping pier at Gathurst. A small pier in Higher Ince fed barges with coal from Ince Colliery, while Ince Hall Colliery seems to have had a pier at Whalleys Basin. Blundell's Pemberton Collieries had a tramway running to a pier near Seven Stars Bridge.

That brings us to the most famous of them all — Bankes's Wigan Pier. The original tramway serving this pier — and itself partly carried on wooden trestle supports — was built for Thomas Claughton in the early 1820s, linking his Stone House Colliery in Goose Green with the tippler on the canal near Wigan Basin. By the 1840s, the line and the pier — along with Stone House Colliery — had been acquired by Meyrick Bankes, and the railway had been extended considerably to link his Winstanley Group of Collieries into the system. The line ultimately ran from Winstanley No 4 colliery, to the No 3 colliery, then to Clapgate pit and, via Stone House colliery, to the canal side at what became known as Bankes's Pier.

Initially the movement of coal tubs on the line was by gravity using inclines when loaded, and horsedrawn back to the pits. After initial mishaps, brake cars were added to the trains — each with six or eight trucks fully laden with coal. By the late 1870s, steam locomotives were being used on the much upgraded railway — fifty years after their use had been pioneered on the lines to Crooke.

The railway and the pier continued in use until well after the First World War but, by the early 1920s, barge carriage of coal was giving way to direct rail carriage. The tippler at the end of Bankes's railway was dismantled in 1929 and sold for scrap. Throughout its life the winches which operated the tipping mechanism were hand-cranked, so there is little likelihood that the operators lamented its passing!

The tippler had gone by the 1930s, but the pier itself — the stone ramp — remained. It became a landing stage for passenger traffic, replacing earlier stages in the Wigan Basin itself.

It was over a period of several years that the area around the canal basin itself became known as Wigan Pier, helped in no small way by the insistence of George Orwell that Wigan Pier didn't exist, and by the now world-wide fame of the Pier itself. By the 1950s, postcards identifying the brick warehouse which is now the Orwell Pub as Wigan Pier had been published, adding to a confusion of claims for the site of the 'original' pier.

So far as researches can ascertain, there are two locations which have a firm claim to be known as "Wigan Pier" — the original Lamb & Moore's tramway which inspired the joke, and Bankes's Pier which assumed the title at the turn of the century.

This small tippler, a reproduction of which is now in position on the ramp, dropped at least 50,000 tons of coal annually into barges, each capable of carrying sixty tons maximum. In round figures, one thousand barge-loads per year were tipped manually from this one site. There are no figures for the total coal loaded on to barges in the Wigan area at the height of local coal production, but it was

considerable. The Crooke Pier could handle larger trucks, and presumably had a much larger annual throughput. Add to those two the many other coal piers in operation in the area and the figures assume considerable proportions.

As we have already mentioned, the pier at Crooke, built some years before Bankes's Pier, was still in use until the 1950s, so coal barges in the canal basin were still a common site long after 'Wigan Pier' was demolished.

Fifty five years after it was removed for scrap, Wigan Pier reappeared, in the form of a reconstruction made by local students. Hopefully, at some time in the future, a short stretch of the tramway can be replaced — and perhaps even supplied with rolling stock — to present a fuller picture of what working life must have been like in Wigan Pier's heyday.

32

32. Wigan Pier, seen here in the 1920s, against the background of an empty canal, was the subject of many local postcards.
Photograph: John Hannavy Picture Collection

33. Everybody liked to have their photograph taken at Wigan Pier — like this chap with a bicycle.
Photograph: Wigan Record Office

34. . . . . and this group of local men
Photograph: Fred Arnold

35. . . . . and these two locals managed to be recorded for posterity on a pre-war postcard.
Photograph: Fred Arnold

36. . . . . a group of participants in the 1934 Wigan Pageant also got in on the act.
Photograph: Wigan Record Office

37. Probably one of the best known of all the pictures of Wigan Pier, this old postcard shows the SS Thomas leaving with a party of trippers. For many people a day spent on the canal on craft like this was the nearest they ever got to having a holiday.
Photograph: John Hannavy Picture Collection

37.

S.S. THOMAS LEAVING WIGAN

38. When Bankes's Pier was no longer required, the decision was taken to demolish it. Demolition was carried out in 1929 by Calderbanks and all the metalwork was removed for scrap.
Photograph: Calderbanks

39. The wooden and metal tippler being hoisted out of position during the demolition work in 1929.
Photograph: Calderbanks

40. Bankes's Pier was just one of several in the Wigan area. This is assumed to be the Pier at Rose Bridge from which coal was loaded on to barges from one of Robert Grant Morris's collieries. Photographed c.1875.
Photograph: Wigan Record Office

40

41. Ince Pier, photographed in the late 1950s.
Photograph: Anthony Grimshaw

42. The coal pier at Douglas Bank Colliery was sited between Crooke and Wigan. This picture dates from about 1880.
Photograph: Wigan Record Office

43. Crooke Pier, photographed in the 1870s. In this picture the pier is not actually in use, despite the heavily laden barge.
Photograph: Wigan Newspapers Ltd

44. Taken at about the same time as the previous picture, this view of Crooke Pier shows tipping actually in progress. A coal truck is held in the tipping mechanism, with its tail flap open.

42   **Photograph: Fred Arnold**

45. Crooke Pier in its last working years — the 1950s. Rebuilt with a much simpler but stronger and more efficient tipping mechanism, the chute is seen here being used to load the barge "Plato".
Photograph: Wigan Newspapers Ltd.

46. The locomotives which hauled the coal trucks to and from Bankes's Pier were all specially built for the job. This photograph shows one of them "Billinge" at the end of the last century.
Photograph: Donald Anderson Collection

47. The line of the old railway linking Bankes's collieries with the Pier can still be seen — now converted into public footpaths.
Photograph by Arnold Hall, Jack Winstanley Collection

48. All ''Shipshape and Wigan Fashion'', Kittiwake stands outside the Mill at the Pier, during the 1983 Inland Waterways National Rally held in the canal basin.
Photograph: Wigan Record Office

Canalside Buildings

The character of a canal is often moulded by the people and places along its banks. Similarly, the lifeblood of a canal comes from the merchandise carried on it.

Both these factors are true of the Leeds Liverpool Canal in general and the Wigan Pier area in particular.

It's well known that coal and cotton were the prime commodities in Wigan's canal economy — the first going outward to many parts of Britain and Europe, the second coming in from even further afield.

A closer look at the canal's history and commercial background shows that as well as coal and cotton it carried a veritable plethora of goods from many parts of the world.

Wigan's commercial canal interests were concentrated on a short stretch from Seven Stars Bridge to the Terminal Building, together with another length running as far as Henhurst Bridge on Chapel Lane. Yet Wigan's influence spread throughout the full length of the canal — from Liverpool to the West and Leeds to the East and to Manchester Docks via the Bridgewater Canal system.

Just as Wigan canal carriers transported goods to probably every one of the 56 main towns served by Britain's longest canal, so Wigan, in turn, received merchandise of every description from them.

The following examples reveal the multiplicity of the goods carried in the bowels of the Leeds Liverpool Canal barges (pulled by horses before the coming of the marine engine) that plied the waterway with such regularity that the water was never still.

Tobacco, sugar, oil, fruits, ham, bacon, butter, cheese, meat, tyres, timber, sacks, cardboard, boxes, flour, paint, chemicals, tea, artificial silk, tin, corn, wheat, biscuits, cakes, hay, potatoes, stone, slate, glycerine, manure, glue, oilcloth (linoleum), cement, agricultural equipment, sand, gravel, rope, twine, gum, cotton, wool, grain, mohair, glucose, paper, bricks, fireclay, dairy produce, laundry machines, grease, needlefelt, steam boilers, beer, cattle food, poultry food, tiles, furniture, calico printing, firelighters, jam, sweets, leather, medical dressings, sheet lead, water pipes, gas tubing, soap, olive oil. All this was set against a backcloth of a waterfront that was flanked by many cotton spinning mills, timber yards, the Soho foundry (in ruins as long ago as 1848), chemical works, several boatyards, limekilns, cokekilns, a flour mill and a pottery. Plus a multitude of cranes dotted about the canal side.

What of the Wigan Pier buildings and their uses? Clearly, those between Seven Stars Bridge and the Terminal Building were originally warehouses designed to receive and hold goods brought by canal, although they were used for other purposes in later years. For example, tyres were once sold from the stone warehouse next to what is now the Orwell Pub at a time when Wigan Pier was, perhaps, at its most unattractive.

We have first-hand evidence about the Terminal Building that stood at the eastern extremity of the canal before the arm leading to Top Lock was built to enable the link with Leeds to be completed in 1816.

Fed by two tunnels at water level, the building was used in two halves. The Pottery Road half was used by H and R Ainscough Ltd., flour millers and produce merchants, the produce including provender for horses. The Wallgate half was worked by H and C Pilkington, produce merchants, who sold cattle food and poultry food.

Ainscoughs were in business in a big way, starting at Parbold in 1837 and at Burscough in 1858. The company had its own fleet of nine canal barges which brought grain from Liverpool and took flour and other produce to Wigan Pier, carrying the coal for their factory on the return journey.

Their boats were named Parbold, Ironclad, Boadecia, Burscough, Victoria, Ambush, Attractive, The Miller and The Pioneer. Two of them, now known as Claymore and Ambush, still run on the canal as passenger boats.

The Terminal Building was still a warehouse for flour and cattle produce during the Second World War. Thomas Pryle, of Marsh Green, now a Wigan postman, recalls collecting sacks of flour and cattle produce for his employers, John Gee and Sons, grocers, of Scholes, in the mid 1940s.

"The sacks weighing 140lb were lifted by hoists from the barges to the various levels of the buildings," he says. "Then they were taken away by wagon or, in some cases, by horse and cart. The flour went to various shops and bakeries in the town and the cattle produce to farms in the area."

There is direct evidence, too, about the brick warehouse that is now the Pier Disco, adjacent to Pottery Road bridge.

William Grindley, of Kitt Green, recalls: "This building was the Cotton Shed for Eckersley's Swan Meadow Mills when I worked there between 1944 and 1947. The difference was that bales of American and Egyptian cotton brought to this warehouse came by road rather than canal because they were too heavy to be lifted from canal barges.

"In contrast, I remember that smaller bales of cotton from South America were delivered by canal barges to the warehouse that is now the Orwell Pub."

On a lighter note, he recalls: "Hot water discharges from Eckersley's Mill kept the canal warm and the lads often took a dip at lunchtime watched by the mill lasses."

The largest canalside warehouse at Wigan Pier is the one that has been converted into the Heritage Centre to provide a base for the museum service. Actually there are two buildings together, both of brick, and they were used to store a wide variety of goods.

The following companies, for example, carried on their businesses alongside the canal between Seven Stars Bridge and the Terminal Building: Webster and Winstanley (stonemasons), Canal Wharves (Canal Transport Ltd.), depot for Tate and Lyle Ltd. (sugar), depot for Fairrie and Co. (sugar), depot for G. and T. Earle Ltd. (cement), H. and C. Pilkington (Produce Merchants), H. and R. Ainscough Ltd. (Produce Merchants and Flour Millers), Taylor Bros. (Victoria Mills), Lancashire Cotton Corporation (Trencherfield Mill).

Trencherfield Mill is one of the very few canal side buildings which today is still used — in part at least — for its original purpose. Three floors of the mill are still used for the manufacture of cotton goods. The ground floor, however, is part of the industrial Heritage complex — housing the world's largest working steam engine as well as museum galleries and an exhibition hall. Also housed in the ground floor are the School of Fashion Studies, and the School of Visual Communication of Wigan College of Technology.

The present mill is the third to stand on the site. Although of twentieth century construction, Trencherfield Mill is very much of nineteenth century tradition — a large mill with canalside access for loading and unloading goods and produce, rather than an adjacent rail link.

That fact demonstrates clearly the importance of the canal well into the twentieth century. Trencherfield was steam powered, and the canal also provided the supply of water for the large triple-expansion engines which powered the mill's machinery.

The earlier mills — Trencherfield No 1 and Trencherfield No 2 — occupied a site to the north of the present building where the car parks now are. No 1 was built in the early nineteenth century, with No 2 being erected in the 1850s. The third mill — the present one — cost the princely sum of £12000 to build.

For the first few years of its existence, it was owned by the Woods family — who also owned the other two mills, and Old Elms Colliery from where coal was produced to fire the mill's Lancashire boilers.

At its peak, the mill employed nearly one thousand people working on eighty thousand spindles, both ring and mule.

By the 1930s the workforce had halved thanks mainly to the new machinery, and today a much smaller workforce still produce textiles within the building.

The mill's main attraction is without doubt the huge working steam engine. The 2000 horse power engines — known as Rina and Helen, with 25″, 40″ and 44″ cylinders and a boiler pressure of 200 lbs per square inch — are brought to life each weekend, turning the huge 26½ft drum which originally carried fifty four ropes taking power to every floor of the building.

Another business that flourished on the canalside, on Swan Meadow Road, was the boat-building concern of James Mayor and Co. Ltd. Founded on the River Douglas at Tarleton, Mayors came to Wigan in 1933 when they leased the workshops of the Leeds Liverpool Canal Company and they remained there until 1959. Their last boat, Darlington, was built in 1953.

Boat builders and repairers, Mayors employed between 20 and 30 shipwrights and engineers and others to make the standard Leeds Liverpool Canal barges, mainly 62 footers. They had oak frames, fashioned on the curve, with straight planks of Douglas fir or pitch pine.

The boatyard had two main slipways, side by side, and boats were launched sideways on.

Harry Mayor, grandson of the founder, still carries on the family business on the Rufford Canal where it joins the River Douglas at Tarleton, four miles from the Ribble estuary. He told us:

"We had some very skilled men at our Wigan boatyard. As well as making boats and repairing others in between orders, we made and tested chains. The canal at Wigan was a busy place."

49

49. We can only assume that "this mon and two lads" were blessed with supreme optimism — it's a long time since fish were caught in this stretch of the canal. The photograph was taken in the early 1950s.
Photograph: Wigan Record Office

50. A typical scene in Wigan Basin in the 1950s. Two barges are being unloaded in the tunnels beneath the Terminal Building, while another waits at the warehouse which is now the Orwell. Note the dockside cranes, now long vanished.
Photograph: Anthony Grimshaw

51. Looking every inch a tidal river, this is the Leeds Liverpool Canal outside the Heritage Centre during the earliest days of restoration.
Photograph: Wigan Newspapers

52, 53, 54, 55, 56. Men and boys prepare for the 1953 launch of "Darlington" — the last boat built at Mayor's boatyard on Swan Meadow Road. Boats were launched broadside into the canal, with spectacular results, as this five picture sequence demonstrates so vividly.

Photographs: Wigan Record Office (52-5) & Private Collection (56)

57, 58, 59. The other end of the line . . . Wigan Basin in the late 1960s, littered with the corpses of many a fine canal boat. Here, among others, lie Plato, Cleo, Bruno and Apollo. Plate 59 was taken from inside one of the tunnels of the Terminal Warehouse, itself occupied by the skeleton of yet another sunken barge.

Photographs by Arnold Hall, Jack Winstanley Collection

57

54

60. Roofless, windowless, lifeless and thoroughly downtrodden, this was the Terminal Building in the late 1950s.
Photograph: Jack Winstanley Collection

61. This photograph was taken at a time when the word "Terminal" could have had a variety of meanings. The scaffolding suggests pending execution — and no one was quite sure if it was meant to hold the building up, or signal its demolition. Now it has new life as "No 1 Wigan Pier".
Photograph: Wigan Newspapers Ltd.

The Restoration

Tempers in the Council Chamber were rising . . . Wigan Pier was on the agenda again. The matter seemed to have been settled once and for all when a leading, influential Councillor declared: "The Wigan Pier buildings are a damned eyesore — we should board 'em up or knock 'em down."

Thankfully, through the wiser counsel of more visionary Town Councillors and, later, of Wigan Civic Trust, restoration overpowered demolition. Wigan Pier was saved by an imaginative multi-million pound operation that will surely immortalise its already world-wide fame.

So what was done to restore the fast-decaying skeleton of Wigan Pier?

The overall blueprint laid down that the new Wigan Pier should be a living, moving, ongoing reminder of Wigan's past rather than a static, stuffy look-but-don't-touch affair. That aim has been achieved by a happy blend of imagination, diligent research, belief in the project, patient but determined application, realism, major surgery and delicate cosmetics.

The Terminal Building has been restored to its original condition and is being marketed as office accommodation rejoicing in the compellingly romantic address "No. 1 Wigan Pier." Once again it stands proudly at the head of the canal complex, as befits Wigan Pier's first building.

The Orwell Pub, in private ownership, has all the trappings of a waterside hostelry on the ground floor — the lounge has direct access to a balcony over the water — and a restaurant and functions room above it. As far as we are aware, the future of the top floor which boasts magnificent original wooden roof trusses, has not been determined.

The smaller adjoining building houses the official Wigan Pier Information Centre and the Pier Shop. On the upper floors is an Education Study Centre where visiting school parties will be briefed before touring the complex or setting sail on various educational cruises.

These start at certain selected points on the canalside (the twin tunnels under No. 1. Wigan Pier, for example) taking in areas of high ecological interest such as Scotman's Flash, Ince Moss and Three Sisters and, in the opposite direction, the delights and the beauty of the River Douglas Valley.

Equally enjoyable, if somewhat less educational, boat trips are available at weekends and these, coupled with the introduction of an Amsterdam-type waterbus plying the pier area three times an hour, promise many animated scenes.

Wigan's past really springs to life in the Heritage Centre which is accommodated in the biggest and most impressive building at the pier. Here the "role play" approach so successful in America harnesses visual and technical aids to tell the story of Wigan in a way that entertains as it informs.

The building itself contains enough of the original fabrication to give the feeling that "another load of merchandise is about to be swung ashore at any moment," while realistic recreations portray the general theme "The Way We Were."

Entering the centre by the smaller of the two buildings is like stepping through the turnstile of a seaside pier. Live actors under the pier provide the sort of Music Hall entertainment so closely associated with George Formby snr. in lively, five minute performances, flanked by the actual Pagefield Siding signal box near which Formby's Wigan Pier joke was born.

Meanwhile, in galleries above and in intimate nooks and crannies, the rich tapestry of Wigan's past unfolds. Under the banner "The Way People Worked" are representations of the working lives of the miner, tinsmith, metal founder, basket weaver, textile worker (especially cotton) and clogger. There are regular demonstrations of basketweaving and the pier has its own full-time real-life clogger.

One gallery houses a complete 1900-style telephone exchange while in another, part of the Park Hotel, a feature of the Market Square area of Wigan for many years, has been reconstructed. Elsewhere, there is a collier's cottage (with outside WC), a Victorian schoolroom where geography lessons are given, a grocer's shop, a chemist's shop, an Uncle Joe's mintballs "factory" and a tripe shop. O, the memories . . .

Situated behind a "shop window" overlooking Wallgate is a moving tableau depicting pit brow lassies screening coal on a conveyor belt, while nearby there is a working model that demonstrates how the coal tippler at Bankes's Pier actually operated.

The history and the attractions spill over on to the canalside outside the Heritage Centre. As well as a rest area for visitors, British Waterways have a waterside garden featuring a canal tug and a lock-keeper's garden patch and varied canal artefacts. The rebuilt stonemason's hut is a British Waterways exhibition and information centre.

Over at Trencherfied Mill, the unique mill engine, in good working order, has already drawn thousands of visitors and remains a big attraction. Believed to be the largest of its type in the world, the engine generates 2,500 hp and has a 26 feet diameter flywheel. Other smaller steam engines are also on display, together with a selection of textile machines making rope and cotton rope.

The Mill at The Pier concert and exhibition hall caters admirably for entertainment and commercial interests, while on the car park outside, a sniff of Wigan's industrial past takes the form of a four-ton steam hammer from Ince Forge.

Now the picture is complete. The reality of Wigan Pier is as famous as the myth.

63

60

64

65

62. The despair and dejection of this scene has now been swept away by the restoration work. The buildings on the right are now the Orwell Pub and the Wigan Pier Information Centre and Shop. The grimy building on the left is now the Pier Disco.
Photograph: Wigan Newspapers Ltd.

63. Trencherfield Mill, and the canal spur arm cut to service it. Trencherfield had no rail link, only loading and unloading facilities for water or road traffic. Kittywake, the barge named after Wigan's Mayoress Mrs Kitty Isherwood is moored alongside several restored steamboats next to the mill.
Photograph: John Hannavy Picture Collection

64. A fine shot of what is now the Heritage Centre in its original role with tarpaulin-covered boats waiting to be unloaded. The brick building (right foreground) has been demolished and the warehouse immediately behind it is now the entrance to the Heritage Centre.
Photograph: Fred Arnold

65. Icebreaking — men and horses were often called into action to try and keep the canal open during hard winters. This scene dates from the 'big freeze' of 1940.
Photograph: Private Collection

66. The turn of a screw by Wigan Council Leader Bernard Coyle and the Wigan Pier Tippler is back — 55 years after being demolished and sold as scrap for £34. On the right is Councillor Peter Hull, Mayor of Wigan when this picture was taken in September 1984. The new tippler was made by students of Wigan College of Technology. **Photograph: Wigan Newspapers Ltd.**

The Ballad Of Wigan Pier

In the knowledge that many places throughout the world owe their fame to a song, Jack Winstanley composed "The Ballad of Wigan Pier." It was recorded on the EMI label by the Houghton Weavers folk group.

The song is intended to preserve the myth of Wigan Pier. Does Wigan have a pier and, if so, where and what is it?

CHORUS

It's long and it's strong and
it leads nowhere,
You can see it when the weather
is clear
If you feel inclined and you've
got the time
You can spend a lovely day on
Wigan Pier

VERSES

Some people say that there's a
pier
In Wigan town somewhere
George Formby said it led t'sands
On stilts up in the air
Some folks'll say that it's a myth
But I don't think that they're
right
'Cos I once fell off yon Wigan Pier
Staggerin' home one night

I've taken part in catchin' tripe
From waters deep and clean
You dangle mint balls on a string
And hope that they are seen
by sticks of tripe that swim around
All shiny bright and new
And just to show where they come
from
There's Wigan written all through

One day I saw the QE 2
Come sailin' up t'Pier
The bunting flew and t'brass
band played
To show the Queen were here
She stepped ashore to thund'rous
cheers
And started to recall
I've seen some piers throughout
the years
But this pier beats 'em all

So if you are told that there's
a pier
In Wigan town somewhere
Don't laugh it off like others do,
Look round you'll see it there
It's spick and span and painted
white
And standin' out a mile
But if you're asked just where
it is
Don't say much, just smile.